Verses
of the
Dusky
Dawn

Verses of the Dusky Dawn

Madhurima Biswas

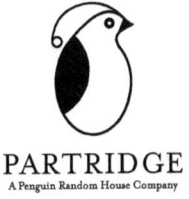

PARTRIDGE
A Penguin Random House Company

To order additional copies of this book, contact
Partridge India
000 800 10062 62
orders.india@partridgepublishing.com

www.partridgepublishing.com/india

Contents

1) Unbroken Promises

"I have spent my days, waiting...
Waiting for you to sink in my hopes..
But there you are.....
Waiting for me to lead on with you..."

It came like the first ray of the dawn..
As it lightened up the treachery slopes
The warbler's call accented the start
like the lilies breakthrough their timid cloves

As, the dawn fell on my dreamy eye....
It seemed like heaven beneath my toes
i exhaled to realize the mighty peaks shine
The warmth of the dawn and the pale cold snow

I remember, those dreary tales of the night
The stories of those black and white morns
Memories, when we decided to make it all right
The colorful goodbyes, screaming out of our broken dorms

Promises are made to be broken, they said

But we will cherish it like our love, we proclaimed

We had cheered with our beers, as we made that pact

Ignoring those judgmental and curious stare

I tell you, i thought we had lost it all

When the tears rolled down on july 10th

I thought, they l retire with the advancing fall

but they decided to stay till the summer, i guess.

Today as i fashion this verse, near the cold edifice

I realize how true our promises stand

The gush of peace and loyalty embraces me

As, The cheers of my mates apprehends my sight

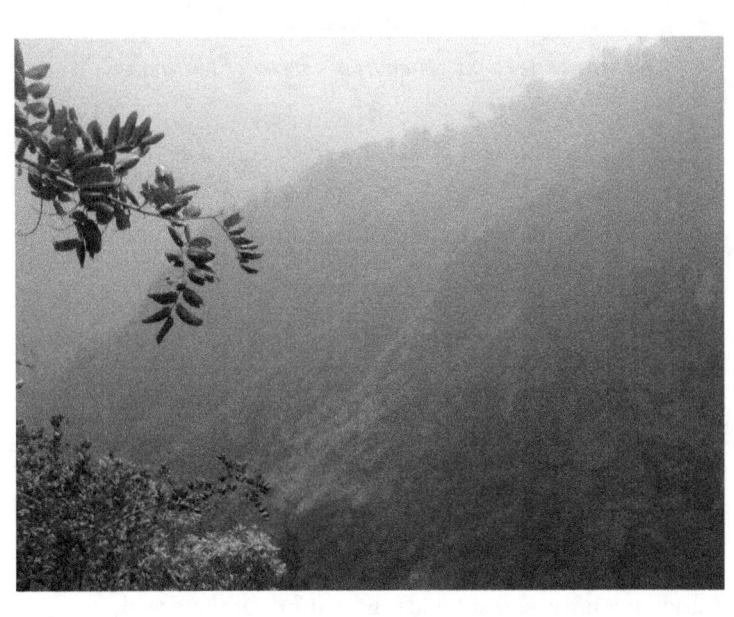

2) Blue Hue Girl

"Eagerness was always her strength..
But sometimes...
Romance see's patience as a Virtue of the brave.."

I saw her Striding past the bouquet shop
Thrilling heat of the winter night fire
Perplexed, by her mighty start
curiosity seemed inviting thy heart

A cup of warm coffee would suffice, i declared
so, thought of visiting an old friend right down the corner
Took my favorite seat beside the warmth of the hearth
but the sight of her passed by my eyes with a startle

She seemed lost in her fiction novel, i guess
spark of her imagination, unraveling instead
There was an aura of intelligence she enslaved
That seemed to make me wonder her present unrest

i could see her patience drifting, i may say
For she seemed to run out of pages to hide
She checked her phone once or twice perse
but unrest had already started its stride.

I wondered which daring heart would have caged her so
Making her question, the decisions, i feel, she dint think
    through
confidence fading with the creases fall
i felt she could recognize the moments judgment call

The next thing i know was a man voice over her cell
Maybe explaining her, the reason for this delay
She seemed to be holding her calmness so
But i could see the sparkles, she quickly tried to hide them
    though

so she kept down the cup, and stood up so tall
i could feel her aura, engaging her in thought
The next thing i heard was the cafe doorbell
And a glimpse of her little blue dress as she passed down the
    lane

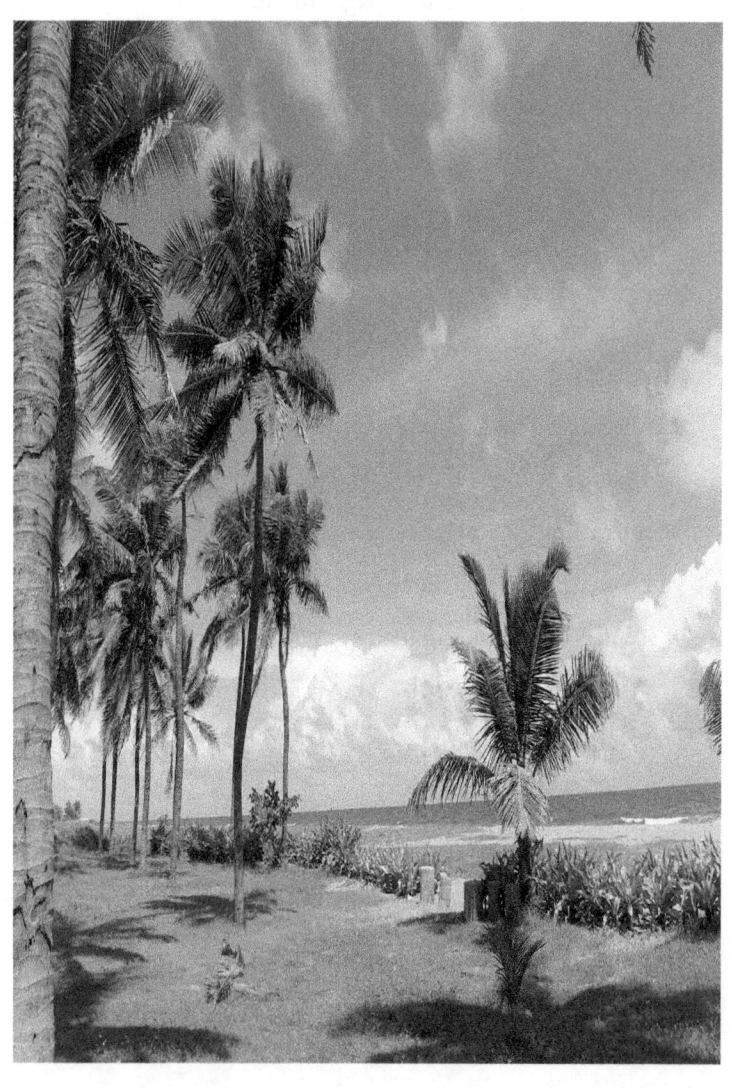

3) Pristine Love

"A love so pure and crude..
knows no bonds and flaws
She will pick you and mold your soul
And teach you how to stride on the virtuous pathway"

A smile on that cold drawn face
like a raindrop on the scorched dry terrain
mesmerizing tears of those mockery and gallows
Didn't seem to suffice her empty heart's salacity and fervors

She had been so feral and vicious
That charm of her eyes eliminating all the adverse
but lately that luxury of bliss had turned to need
For, she craved for a mild palm to be led by her dire breed

She prayed and prayed almost distressing her soul
Crying and reaching out to all those wealthy spiritual, foes
I don't know it was magic or pagan deeds to explain
but those bits seemed to paying their resultant heed, not slain

For, she learnt she was at last the blessed,

To be bearing the sign of love in her womb

The love of her life had thus embedded thy seed

To let her know that she isn't to be lost as the soul of the tomb

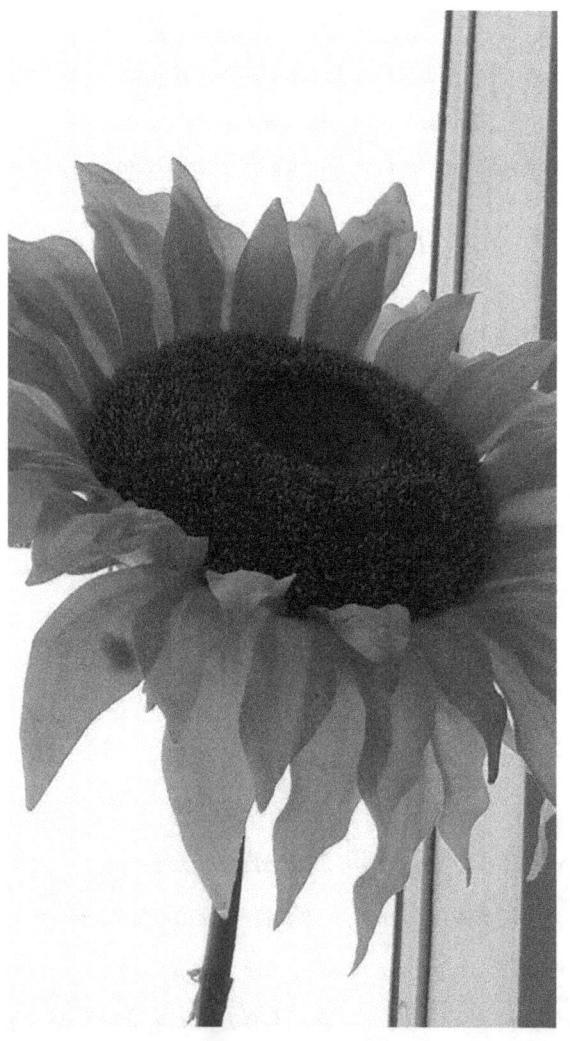

4) Dainty Hearts.

"flame relinquishes flame
But is evanesced only by the humble rain"

Is this our dream abode?

A question, i choose to ponder on

Humanity has hit its fateful abate, i say

I wonder why, why there is so much hate?

Wasn't love the only word preached by our Lords in different
ways?

The violence of Syria, Rome and Kashmir

Everyplace seems to scream the hour of peace

Blood of kids, wives and men, Seem to drench the streets with
the unsaid dreams they once salvaged

They preach to create a world of honor, hopes and dreams

And all we witness is this dire need of regret.

The kids lost their lives under our creators guild

What do we teach our bairn hereon?
To lose faith and wait for the fates call?

We mold them to learn the art of integrity and grace
Their look awaiting for just a small gesture of assurance
The assurance of protection and freedom
but, i doubt, needs like these have now become quite seldom
Don't give them hopes, false to be precise
Don't teach them the art of submission and compromise
Teach them the art to tackle hate, very young, i dread
For this day is more about healing the wounds of the scarred.

I see them looking outside the pane each morn
awaiting for the morning dew to drench the yard.
Those eyes of dreams, hopes and success
but hearts full of fear, sorrow and lament

Love and peace walk hand in hand
Teach them to nurture affinity to one soul and land
teach them the art of care and prayer
for they are the dainty soldiers to save us from the fated end.

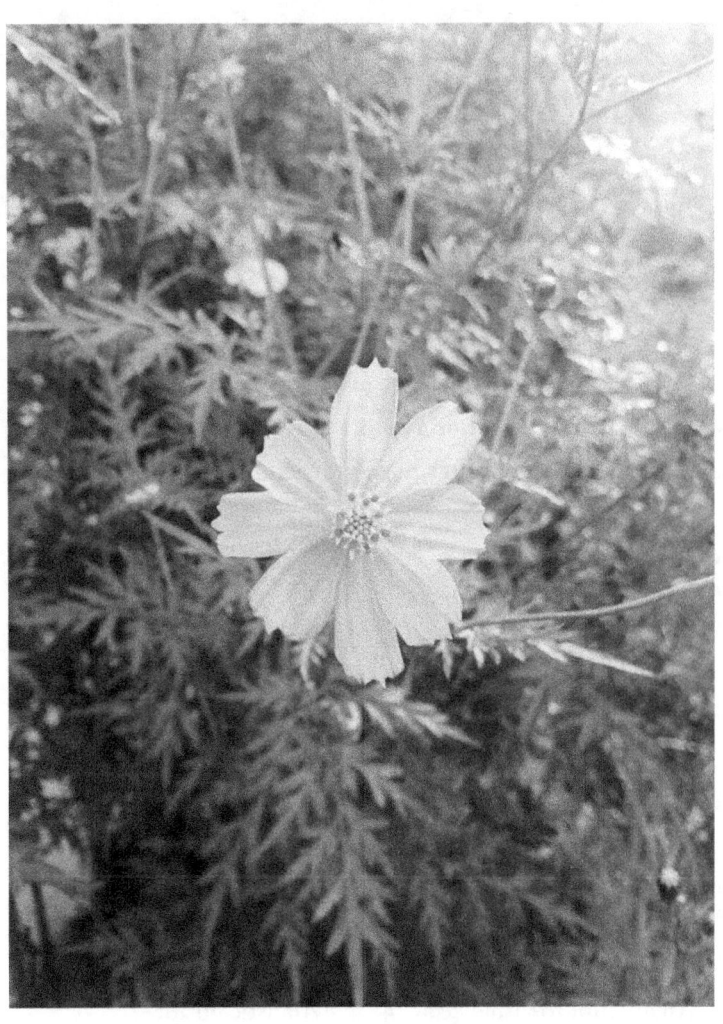

5) Perfection of Art

"They will love you for your attire..
They will disguise your soul
They will materialize your desire..
They may become your foe...
They may hold you back..
Teach you the art of the world..
But perfection is not a predefined form...
but a beauty with grace and hope..."

She urges to be a perfection of art

Trying her best to suffice her soul

Drooling for the love of long lost part

But not knowing the truth that stands pretty bold

Staring at oneself in the mirror

She tried to peek at the reflection of future

An attempt to visualize at the materialistic horror

but doesn't that seem vague near the prescribed nurture?

She remembered her teenage struggles
trying to define herself by the so called rules
The way she had discovered, outer shape was primary for any
    strong groove

She wondered if he would accept her so
now that her cast may change
But insecurities had always been her foe
and, Trust had always seem so strange.

She decided to let go of the flaws
Trying to look into ones eyes in the mirror
Searching for some confidence and peace
for the call sounded her love's patience

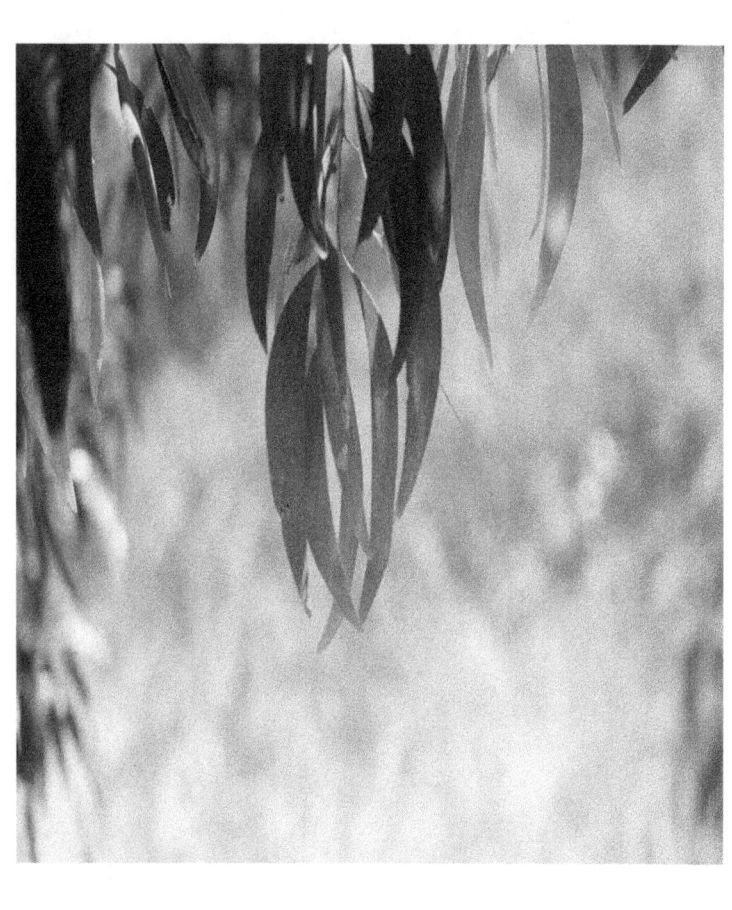

6) City Lights

"Blinking above..
Leading you on..
Know what is true and what is drawn..
Let it shine...let it glow...
They will stay..
Forever...no matter who sins your soul.."

The city lights, seem distant by the beat
It soothes the dismay that fills thy soul
Sworn to bestow the warmth in this cold street
As we pass by embracing destiny's fateful role

I sit here, staring at those brown passionate eyes
Wondering what you search in those glimmering road beside
Passion engulfed in shy and pretty smile of glee
Exclaiming the love cloven among this dark wishful night

I wonder of all the moments to come,
Whether they will present smiles or sorrow

Whether acceptance would be my choice
Or compulsion dreading me to embrace the morrow.

I wish to leave this moment here
Not to disrupt its peaceful ambience
Its seems like a dreadful prayer
To yearn for love when i have been granted the cradle so
     pristine.

I have laid my cards, all my losses and strength
All my wounds of the past lay vulnerable, seeking you
i lay my worries in your humble endearment
these city lights seem to sniggle and fade away....

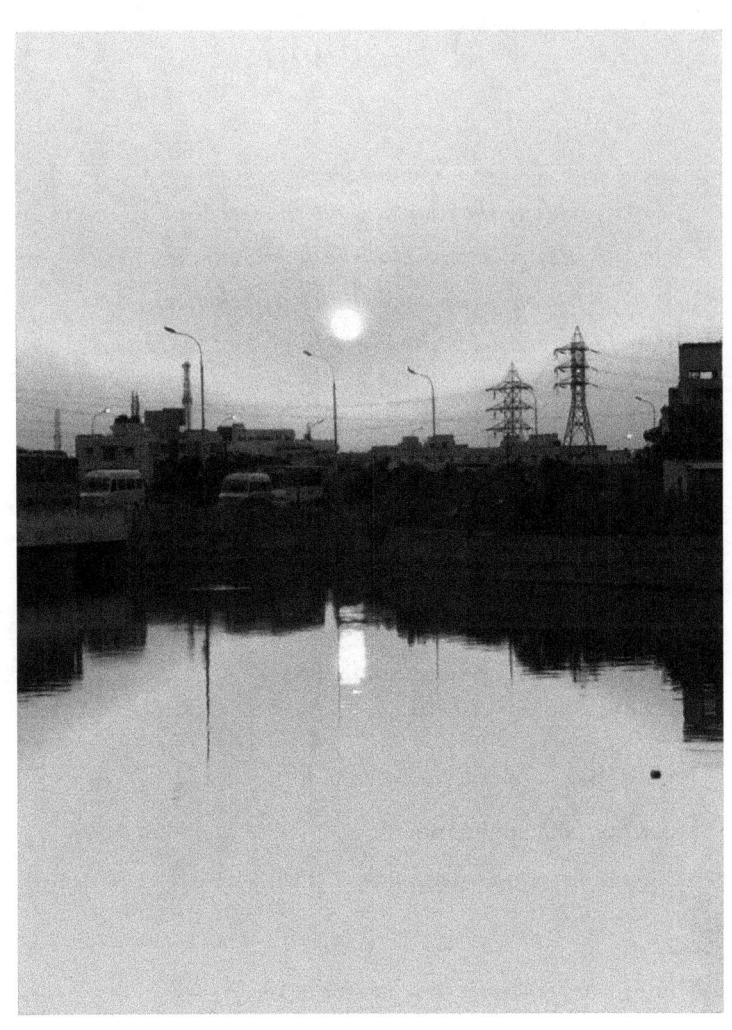

7) Lead On..

"Roads run..
Along the coast.. along the terrain..
along the forests and along the snow..
But they run...they don't seek shelter..
For if they rest...Their essence fades and fades.........."

Beneath the cold thin air
There seems to be a paradise of hope
Beside the muddy tardy street
There lies a land of promise and scope

Time is they say a task supposed to heave and ho
Apart from the mighty tides
Expectations lies to pave and cave aboard

Minimal desire resides in a meager heart
Evitable enough but inevitable declares the mind
Each step is cautious but why doesn't it seem right?
A strand of hay seems enlightening the more

May be that is the conclusion of the nature s drool

A warm word on doorstep seems to strengthen the cold floor.

May be a faded ray of hope is the destiny for humanity to look
up for.

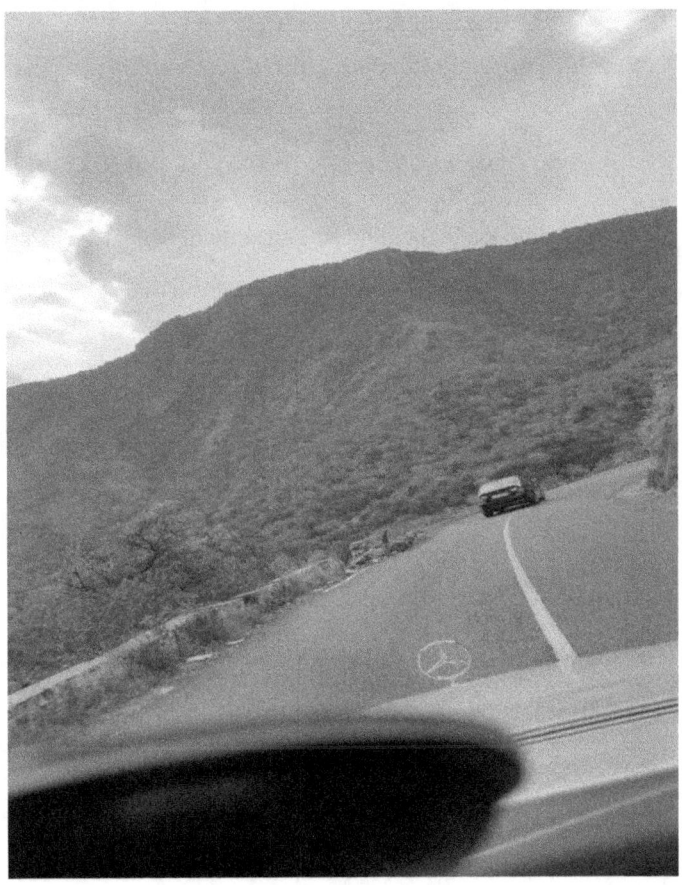

8) Sparkling Lights

"I would follow the light i see..
it shines so bright, guided by thee.."

There are million stars sheltering us on
The city deep down engulfing every painful past
It seems they don't want to reveal ones mood
But there those stars shine...shine their way to the mysterious moor

City lights seem bright...bright but ...impromptu unlike the
gleaming sunlight..
They shine.. but are reserved only to moments at hand..
For they will wear out soon ..much sooner.. before you realize
their feeble might...
But the stars shine...shine their way to the end of mortal life...

City lights seem lasting.. last but not like the callous dims above,..
They enlighten but not wander with the human aggressive
mind..

For they are stagnant.. much because you aren't apt for holding
them on..

But the stars shine..shine with you wherever your sway even
though without your kind...

Realize just realize there may be clouds..

many clouds and snow but once it all parts they l again come
and embrace your though...

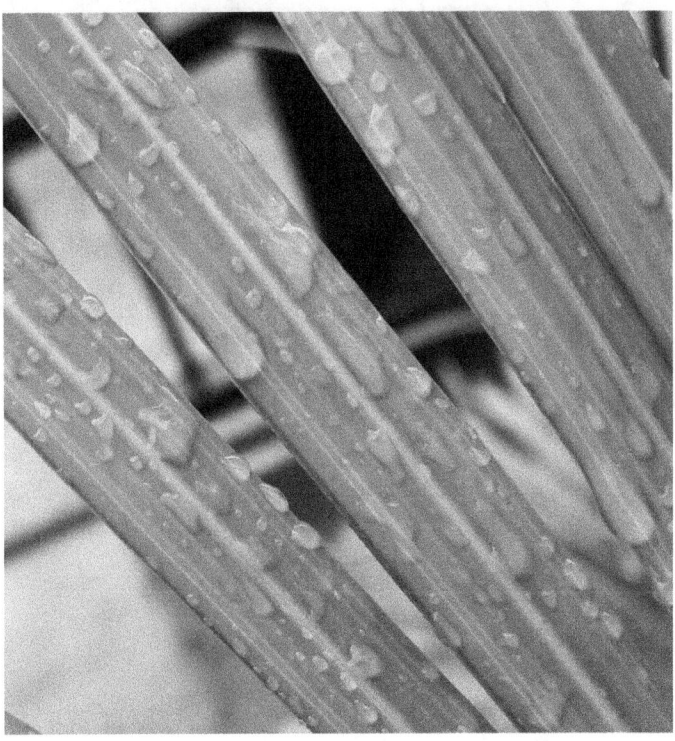

9) Dawning of Passion

"Our romance doesn't fade..
It doesn't depend on our mortal self..
Even if this is the last breath i embrace..
Know, my Love, our passion wouldn't
diminish even in a million decades......"

I looked up to that light..

Gleaming with this moment's aura..

Trying to look behind

Those deep forsaken mysterious enigma

You once had narrated

The identity of your soul's seigneur

The dreams it beholds and the lusty, brisk hope

I had held your hand, not to let go i thought

Thus letting the deep rooted insecurities settle off

Your touch reminded me of the Romeo's grace

Promising, dreamy and the earnest embrace

The charcoal soon was dismissing its warmth

But it wasn't what my heart had sought

Ocean s depth couldn't have defined this criterion

It held its breath to uproot the manacle

I sat there trying to pile the flaws.

But all my heart could do was applaud

For your touch has been engraved, my love

Disdain and doubts now seemed like foes

Lifting my heart up and exclaiming thy win

All i seek was your dawning intent

Insecurities dint seem to shine that while

For it seemed to vague thy dim fiery light

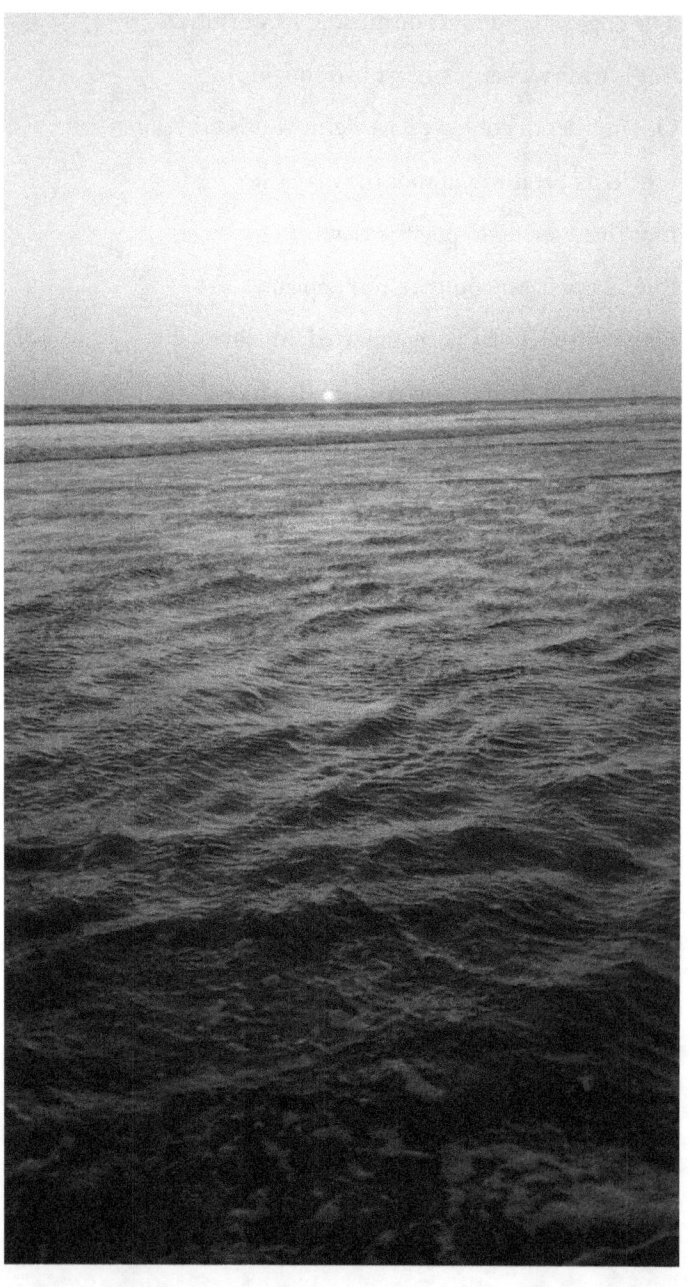

10) The Last Lullaby

"last is when we define it to be..
lets not regret rebate our peace..
every moment is our last if we see..
for humble is this life.. no matter how
hale you mold it to be"..

She enclosed a stormy heart and a summer soul
craving her way through the darkest enclaves
strolling her way through her doubtful fogs
leaving them behind, but did she know?

This is a wild goose chase, a wild forest of creeps
deepens the fears of the weak and threatens the strength of
the might
but she kept going, for it was that old song leading
That song! that radio song of 1959.
She followed and followed and the dusk was falling
she believed she would find it, but did she know? it wasn't that
old winter fog?

I wanted to tell her, all i had learnt about this age from the
    west,

to let her know that its no more a land of dreams and flakes

to tell it it isn't her choice to lead on and slog

for the dreams she had once believed were long and long gone

i tried...trust me i did...i screamed...intensity elevating with the
    hopeless heart pounding

Shouting and running i ran behind her, touched her wind her
    mighty wind

it slashed the failing heart that i had saved inside.

i pulled her,,, trying to bring her back.. but there she was, not
    caring even for this broken lad

i begged her to wait to just turn and see.. at last............she
    turned saving me from the fallen heap

she turned and looked.........................i can't explain how
    magical she was!!!

full of life...and oh those sparkling dreamy eyes!.

i looked and looked ..kept staring at her will..

but then she touched my chest and the hopeless heart seemed
    beating!

Trying to soothe the wounds that had long been befallen...

"You have courage to protect this heart....let the beat lead you
to the aspirations of that night..

Go where it takes...but leave the fears with me....love with it
all....but drown the doubts that you achieve............

and i promise.....when the day comes, for, heart to stop and
rest forever...

the radio will play the same song that once made your heart
restless and fierce

*... **but that day my love...it will be** t**he last lullaby**,*

for the memoirs of these deeds will enchant your dreams
forever!

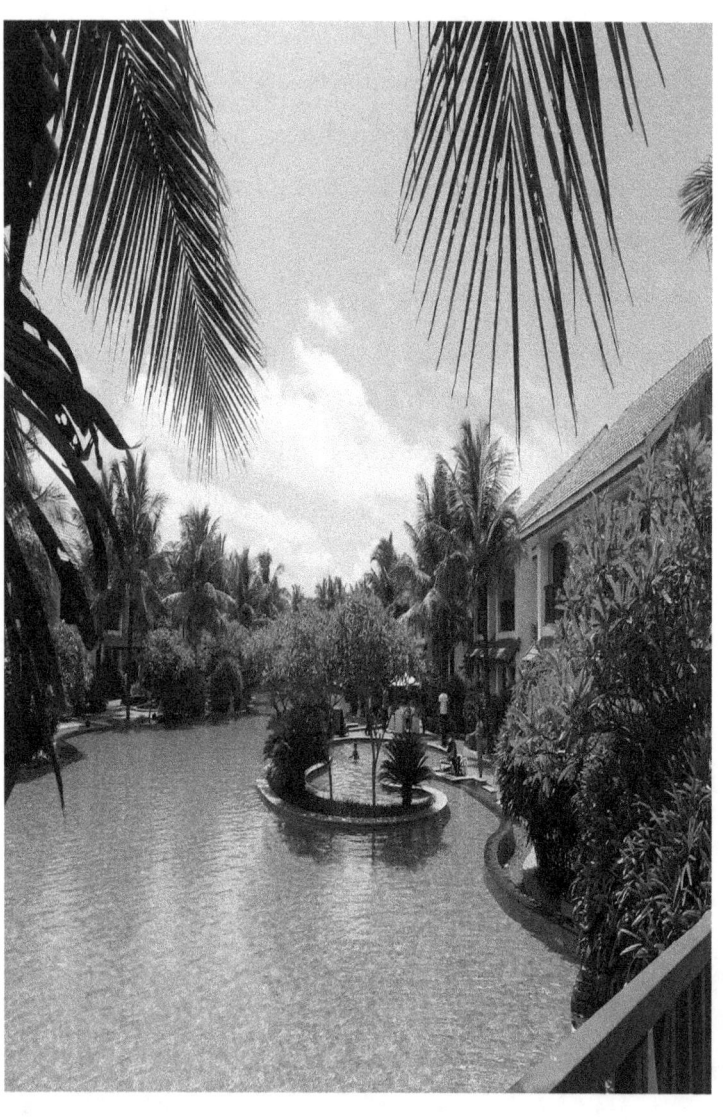

11) Weather of Peace

"I won't let nature...
diminish our shine...
i won't let this world..
define our hopes mild..
This rain would dry..
and peace would lose vigor..
But dreams of the humble never lose the fervor"

So many nights of endless worries

So many days of faithful companies

So many smiles hiding painful memories

So many hearts crying of misery

So many tears awaiting to fall

So many steps trembling for scars

So many thoughts of faith and hope

So many commitments pulling us back though

I strive to push through this lane of delusion

Trying hard each day to stride along further

Keeping my head high and hiding my fervor

Conscious of what the world declares in my favor

Tired of accepting destiny's different verdict

Tired of beholding the temporary fading agony

Tired to letting go the ones i always adored

Tired of promises assuring not to let go

But its been always this way isn't it?

We have learnt to live in a world of ephemeral needs

But lets not forget my dear friend, a heart to heart bond is
    forever made of strength

Promises are just an aid of assurance my dear

But lets forget these anguish and fear

For this day is pristine..pure and primal

Turn around and inhale this weather of peace

Just look up.. and let this rain scour this pain and need.

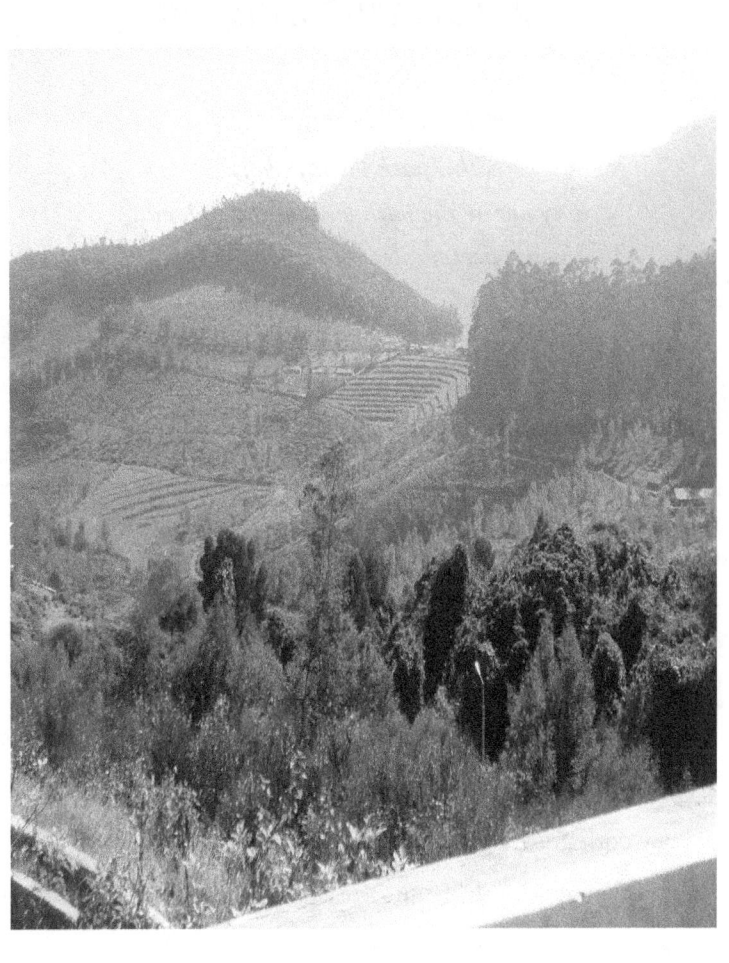

12) Evident Change

"This path i advance on..
this path i embrace..
may not be the path we wanted to lead..
let me declare, let the destiny speak...
this path would always lead to you and me.."

There lies this thought

Beneath the rules..

That questions facts and silent blues..

A thought of wisdom ..warm and bright..

But quite different from the methodical lies.

Nature and man are not far apart..

They both grow together from the start..

They change with the coming seasons of faith...

Warm and sunny in the times of mirth..

Suddenly they shift their course that goes astray..

Through the rivulets of storm and pray...

Men and nature are bound to change...

Even if we decide to frame them straight...

Fixation doesn't define them though..

So let them change and allow them to grow..

Commitments and promises.. may stomp their advance...

So allow them to self discard their trance...

They l find a way to grow and shine....

All they need is our support and might!

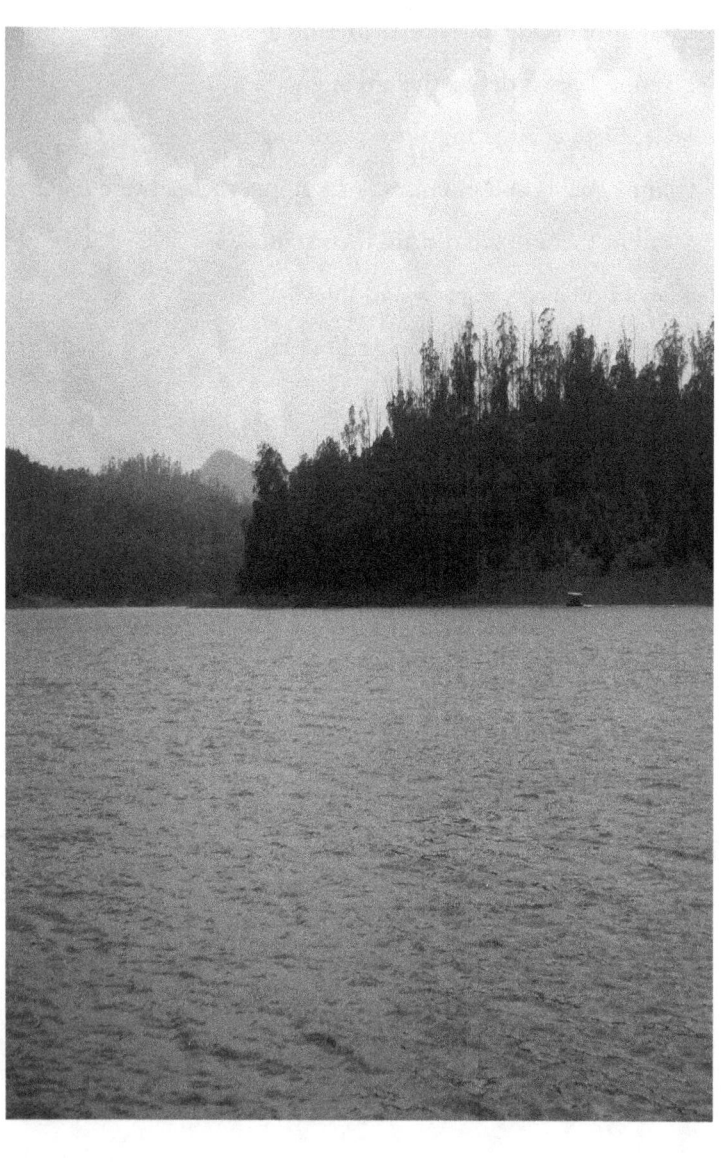

13) Unique You

"Wanderlust...may cruise uphill or downhill..
but it would lead me to the lands that hold
the mysteries of the untold truth"..

Build up a heaven

Spark it along hopes

Live it up to the moment

And is that how it goes?

We create a future

A future of dreams

A dream of zee s our loved ones

Walking beside with broken hopes

They tell us to let go

Leave it up and live in the day

I decide to drag some miles more

But that isn't a decision of my own

I walk for some more miles

But that doesn't seem right

Why do in rules we all subside?

We intend to create a place anew

And here we are a few among this endless queue

That rebellious self that once we harnessed

Doesn't seem to portray in this hour

We tend to follow the predefined judgment

Assuring that it is the right thing for sub missing the scars

Lets not forget. Creation is judgmental

Lets not succumb to those questioning eyes

Lets allow ourselves to high rise and fall

And lets not forget history has been made by these creative
tries!

15) Lady in the Bar

"The smooth satin glow..
engulfed the truth that she would behold..
Her vigor and might..
Claimed to be the deity of the silent night."

A pretty red gown of satin
Lined with the humble lace
A face so sculpted and plain
Would never leave your heart without a trace......

She enters the stoned dark enclave.
With nothing but a lonesome attitude
A lonely sight of beauty that enslaves
but lacks the greatness of gratitude....

All eyes turn as her stilettos click
Penetrating the scorching attention
As she searches for a seat with the sexy hair flick...
Besides the bar and thus handles the lonesome pain....

All the people looking intently
She ignores all the unwanted sight
Dint seem that she demands randomly..
rather than her favorite scotch by her side.....

She waited for an hour and a half i guess..
when a bartender slipped a card
She gave a read as she accessed
And diligently walked up as i witness...

She headed to the reception they say
All the eyes following as the lady departs
Went to the elevator with a deep intent look
As i finally caught the sight of those dark demanding eyes!

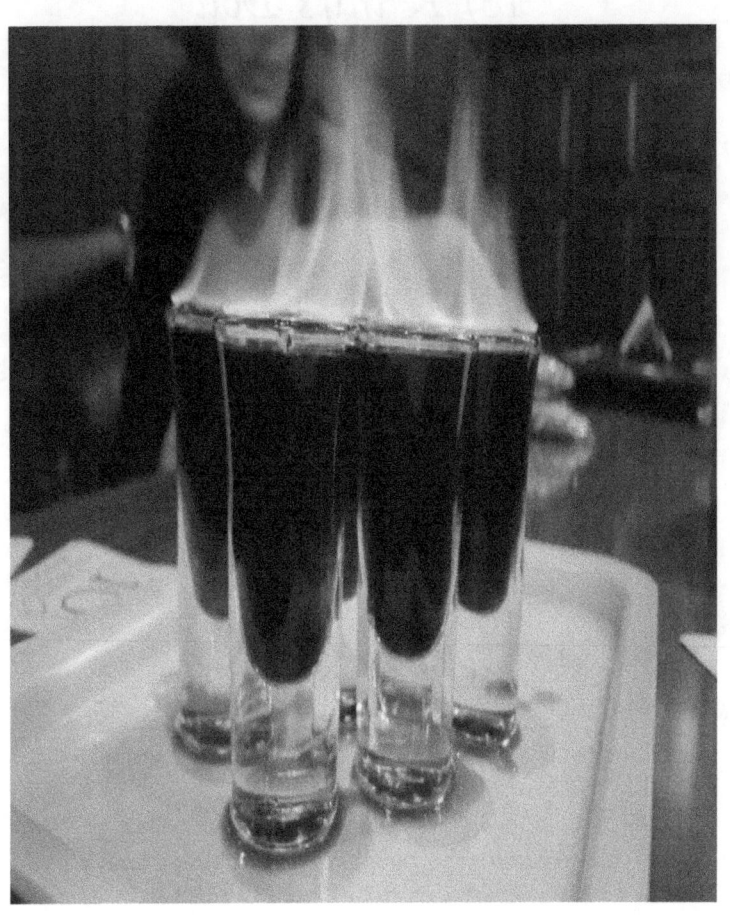

16) Penny's Doll

"He had promised to return with a smile..
But she saw his radiance brighten this inevitable light"

"Get me a dolly papa, promise me you will,

for i have seen Ellie›s superior grin

Its a cute little dolly laces pink, purple and blue

It wears a furry green coat, and oh! yea those glittery yellow
shoes"

papa seemed to know now, the dolly penny wanted,

but mommy seemed to look all teary and stranded

"but mommy, why dont you convey to papa the dolly you
desire,

dont you remember he bought jacky, the last time i had
enquire?"

Mommy dint find it a good idea, i guess

but penny knew, papa always kept the promises true to witness so she ran alone the steps with a message for farewell at heart

"mommy?papa will come back, why do you always drench his
depart?"

Its been a while, two weeks to be sure..

mommy seems to ignore penny and love the picture box more

but one day, a friend came and told penny to rejoice

because papa will be back, with the dolly he had promised a
while back

but litlle did penny know, this dolly is tough to find

for dolly had no mood to come to a penny s kind.............!!!!

So, penny pulled up her skirt and fetched her darling piver,

for she thought those loud shots outside, would startle and
make him shiver..

"pivi, just those people playing loud you know?

didnt mommy tell you..it is how the big people learn to grow?"

Mommy seemed to think the game wasnt that good, i think

because penny saw her mommy stumble her way to the porch
like the blinding wind..

"mommy mommy, dont run, pivi will get more scared, mommy
please..

why would you do this when you already know he is scared of
  that dark breeze..

penny ran out, and saw mommy sitting down.
"mommy again you are teary, doesn't papa tell you these drops
  make him frown?
mommy seemed to ignore whatever penny said..
but all of penny' s concern was drowed by piver and the rest..

Then penny saw, that motionless person beside..
looked like papa, but why does his eye shut so tight?
"papa what's wrong? exclaimed penny on and on..
but papa dint seem to notice.(she thought)..... that its ok for
  him to bring the dolly next fall!

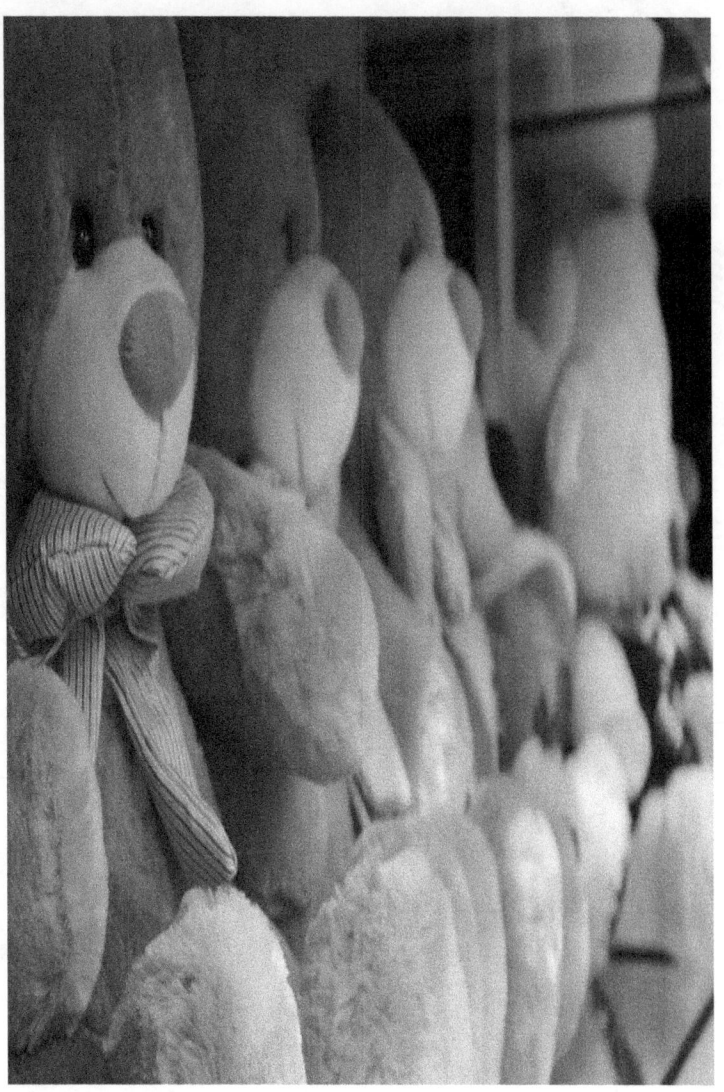

17) Transient Romance

"Let her fly..
let her shine..
let her go..
but not into the night..
let him hold..
let him lead..
but let her know..
Its not forever they need.."

She was sitting beside the window.

In deep thoughts, i guess

She seemed to be thinking for hours together.

The rain didn't seem to bother her.

Nor did the frizzy hair

All she could think about

Was the moments to follow and forgive her unrest

She remembers the first day she met him

He seemed like a normal old boy

Hidden behind the tattered book
"What is it so special about the Nazis?
That he doesn't bother to play with us instead?"
She seemed to ponder about it for a while
But her mate's eagerness declined the moment's shine

Marking her performance's peak, was her main aim
"Maybe after the game, i will enquire him about his unique
    interest?"
She was not a person to attend such a demand
But she had felt familiarity with this new lad

She knew they have not yet started to play together
But she mentally addressed him as he friend, she thought..
    why bother?
Mother says friendships last forever and ever
"I believe her, no matter what my stupid sister says."

....

They came, with your beautiful dress my child
jewel of gold and diamonds and what not i say!

Lots of savories and sweets to make the days
And oh! what beautiful ornaments, i have to state.

Theirs must be a beautiful heart my girl
For these mountains have heard the tales of the broken
But he seems to be guy of promise
And his people, a clan of respect and faith

I don't know why, i was against your wish
You seemed to have grown up my lady
A beauty in your heart and mind rests
And a smile, to forever adore His finest artistry.

Your father, was proud to see their grace and virtue
The way they paid respect to our Great
They seem to follow the deeds of the pure
For they promised to, nourish you with nurture and praise

You have to smile my dear girl
Why does your eye portray sorrow?
This is the night for your endearment
Not for those tears to mark their way to the morrow.

....

She heard the words of her beloved mother

As the tears had found their way

She lay there against the pane

Subletting the rain to take her to the land far away.....

It was middle school, i guess

He had told me about his dreams and passion

It portrayed the spark behind his eyes

That liberated his soul from all the expectations and distress.

He used to speak about the oceans and seas

How they made him feel the freedom, he so pleased

She felt safe, in his mysterious eyes

Though they never promised her hopes and dreams

She used to travel back after play

but unlike others, it made her sad

those tides seemed strange to her day by day

but her village's library knew it all, she hoped and claimed.

She would ransack all the shelves

In search of the mighty storms that waves unfold

He would talk about crossing shores

That embarks the colors the world enfolds.

Next day, she went, waited for dusk to fall

And once it fell, there was no sight of his precious face

She waited for days and weeks i guess..

Till the leaves hugged the earth and we welcomed the spring.

One day she heard some one say,

He had been missing from the day they last played

waves from the west have washed away their abode, they claim

"but he is a humble comrade of the waves" to them she explains.

....

She woke up with a start

As the clock tower struck the midnight bell

She looked around to witness

A bouquet of fresh lilies by the bedside dresser.

....

It had been a good harvest that year

Father seemed to be happy, this time

There was a celebration for the whole clan

As it was not a regular sight of four bags, rice and hay.

Mother had sent her to fetch wood from the shed nearby

Where she was caught by some unusual sight

Someone seemed to have messed with her stack of logs

Unaware of her wrath that may soon befall

He turned and smiled

Her wrath seemed to subside

She looked at him for a while

Trying to recognize this familiarity in disguise

She knew that smile

She had been searching for this glee

She had searched for this peace

That had once gotten away

"Where were you so long?", she exclaimed

But her question turned into a scream of despair

She stepped forward for a violent embrace

And let this moment hold the passion's grace.

....

"Wake up, dear angel", dawn has arrived

Its your day, your time and your might

The long awaited moment of dreams and hopes
has dawned with the rays of serenity and peace

She opened her eyes, to the kiss of present
The gleam of the sunrise, striking the snowy hill
The chirp of the birds, taking flight of the dawn
Warming her heart, and pleasing the torrid bleak

Bejeweled eyes, rosy lips
Attire of beauty, glamor and bloom
Resembled the awakening of that forsaken broken moor

She had dreamt about this morn
The moment she would be THE ONE
the one who sparkles his heart
and flames it with zeal and amour

Enduring smile
passionate eyes
A love so true and pure
Mirth of sun and rose's thorn
Seem to be emerging in this moment's glow

....

She was dressed in royalty, they said
It was like a dream come true
A love so pure and patient
deserves a bestowal of a golden hue

She rested in her room, shy and smile
witnessing the moment's patient glow
Suddenly, she heard wails, not laughter
Which raced her heart instead.

Standing tall, and flying like the thundering storm
Unleashing her braided hair
She stumbled among those carpet, still warm
From the last week's chatter and jovial flair.

There lay her Romeo, but those eyes didn't shine
Nor did those lips enslave a passionate smile
Nor did he bequeath roses and tulip
Nor did he hold her hand to lead and assist

Nor did she feel that passion and love
Nor did her future sparkle, like those star's above
Nor did she feel the need to dream again
As she witnessed her life fade away.............

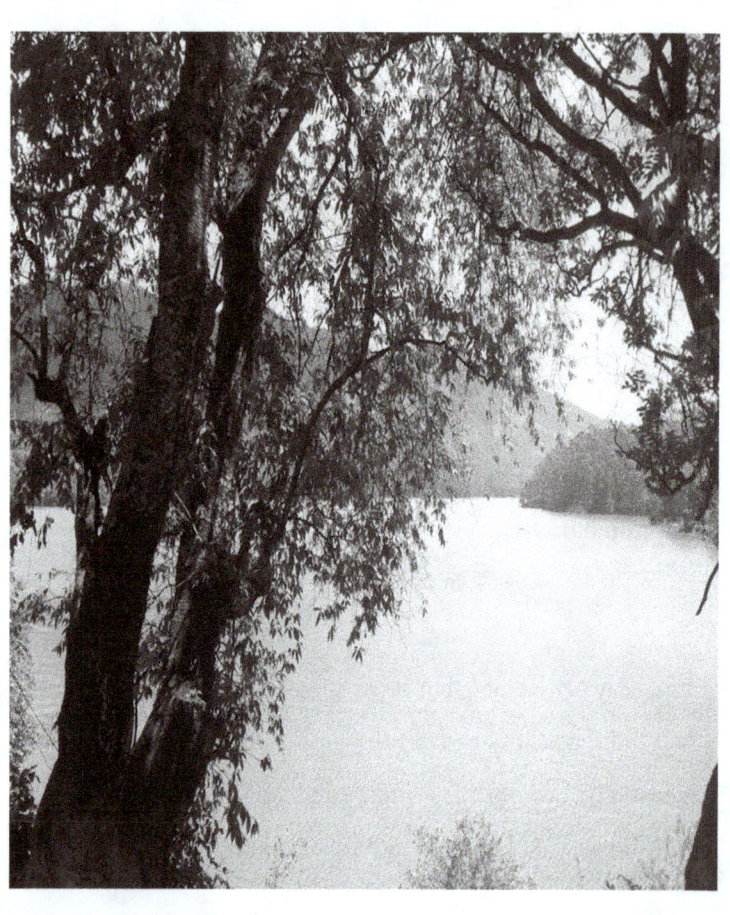